Neo-Platonism

Theosophical Publishing Society

Kessinger Publishing's Rare Reprints

Thousands of Scarce and Hard-to-Find Books on These and other Subjects!

- Americana
- Ancient Mysteries
- Animals
- Anthropology
- Architecture
- Arts
- Astrology
- Bibliographies
- Biographies & Memoirs
- Body, Mind & Spirit
- Business & Investing
- Children & Young Adult
- Collectibles
- Comparative Religions
- Crafts & Hobbies
- Earth Sciences
- Education
- Ephemera
- Fiction
- Folklore
- Geography
- Health & Diet
- History
- Hobbies & Leisure
- Humor
- Illustrated Books
- Language & Culture
- Law
- Life Sciences
- Literature
- Medicine & Pharmacy
- Metaphysical
- Music
- Mystery & Crime
- Mythology
- Natural History
- Outdoor & Nature
- Philosophy
- Poetry
- Political Science
- Science
- Psychiatry & Psychology
- Reference
- Religion & Spiritualism
- Rhetoric
- Sacred Books
- Science Fiction
- Science & Technology
- Self-Help
- Social Sciences
- Symbolism
- Theatre & Drama
- Theology
- Travel & Explorations
- War & Military
- Women
- Yoga
- *Plus Much More!*

We kindly invite you to view our catalog list at:
http://www.kessinger.net

THIS ARTICLE WAS EXTRACTED FROM THE BOOK:

Theosophical Siftings: A Collection of Essays

BY THIS AUTHOR:

Theosophical Publishing Society

ISBN 076612990X

NEO-PLATONISM.

A Lecture read Before the Chiswick Lodge of the Theosophical Society, February 26th, 1894.

Neo-Platonism—that is, New Platonism—is, essentially, much the same thing as Old Platonism. It is the name given to the body of doctrines professed by a school of philosophy which arose at Alexandria during the third century of the Christian era. This philosophy was based, as its name declares, upon the teachings of Plato, and more particularly, upon the mystic, or esoteric, aspect of those teachings. By modern scholars, with one brilliant exception, the writings of the Neo-Platonists have been almost completely ignored. Commentators upon Plato, whose whole equipment consists in a more or less competent knowledge of the Greek grammar, will tell you that what the Neo-Platonists did, was, to obscure the clear meaning of their master under a veil of fanciful and generally absurd mysticism. It is permissible, however, to doubt whether Plato's meaning be quite so clear as some of these grammatical persons suppose. Aristotle studied it for twenty years, and it is by no means sure that he clearly understood it, even then.

Plato derived his learning from many sources. He was, as you know, the pupil of Socrates. After the death of his master he studied, under Cratylus, the system of Heracleitus the obscure. Next, he went to Italy, where he learned the doctrines of Pythagoras; and Pythagoras, says Madame Blavatsky, "obtained his knowledge in India, or from men who had been there."[*] At a later date Plato journeyed to Egypt "for the purpose," says his biographer, Olympiodorus, "of conversing with the priests of that country; and from them he learned whatever pertains to sacred rites." That is to say, in Egypt he was initiated. And lastly, travelling into Phœnicia, he learned there the science of the Magi. Thus he became acquainted with the occult wisdom of India, of Egypt, and of Persia.

In the writings of Plato, therefore, this occult wisdom may be discovered, by those who possess the Key; for, in the words of *Isis Unveiled*, "every time the subject touches the greater secrets of the Oriental *Kabala*, secrets of the true cosmogony of the universe, and of the *ideal*, pre-existing world, Plato shrouds his philosophy in the profoundest darkness."[†] With

---

[*] *Isis Unveiled*, Vol. I, p. 9
[†] Vol. II. p. 39.

the immediate disciples of Plato, the knowledge of his esoteric meaning passed away, not to be revived for several centuries. "This task," says Thomas Taylor, the Platonist, "was reserved for men who were born indeed in a baser age, but who being allotted a nature similar to their master were the true interpreters of his sublime and mystic speculations. Of these Plotinus was the leader, and to him this philosophy is indebted for its genuine restoration, and for that succession of philosophic heroes, who were luminous links of the golden chain of deity."* These "philosophic heroes" were the Neo-Platonists, of whom I am now to speak. I propose, therefore, in the first place, to give you a very brief historical account of the Neo-Platonists themselves, and after that, to attempt some slight examination of the doctrines which they promulgated. In quoting from their works, I shall make use of the translations by Thomas Taylor, whose life-long and enthusiastic services to the cause of Platonic philosophy must always be remembered, by every true Platonist, with feelings of gratitude and admiration.

The foundation of the Neo-Platonic school is ascribed to Ammonius Saccas, a working-man of Alexandria, who died, at a very advanced age, in the year 243 of the Christian era. But we know very little about Ammonius. He was the son of Christian parents. Porphyry tells us that he renounced Christianity: certain of the Christian Fathers tell us that he did nothing of the kind. I should be inclined, on more than one account, to take Porphyry's word for it, but it may be possible in some measure to reconcile these opposite statements. Ammonius, it cannot be doubted, held, as modern Theosophists hold, the great doctrine of the fundamental unity of all religions. He found it necessary, as many since his time have found, to abandon the forms of Christianity; getting rid of the husks, as it were, to arrive at the kernel; renouncing *a* religion, to attain religion itself. Thus even in separating himself from the Christian Church, he might be said to remain a Christian in the esoteric sense.

But the most important thing we have to remember respecting Ammonius, is, that one day, while he was lecturing in his school at Alexandria, a young Egyptian entered the school, brought thither by a friend. This young man was a student of philosophy; he had already attended one of the many schools then flourishing in Alexandria, and had got very little satisfaction out of it. After listening for some time to Ammonius, he turned to his friend, and exclaimed, "This is the man I have been seeking!" He immediately attached himself to Ammonius, and remained in Alexandria for eleven years as his disciple. The name of the young student was Plotinus.

* Introduction to the Select Works of Plotinus, p. 8.

In one of his essays, Mr. Walter Pater has a fine sentence about Plotinus. He calls him "that new Plato, in whom the mystical element in the Platonic philosophy had been worked out to the utmost limit of vision and ecstasy." This is not only finely said, but very truly said. Plotinus inaugurated for us a new era of Platonic interpretation. How much he owed to Ammonius we cannot tell; for the writings of Ammonius, if he *did* write, are not now extant. The works of Plotinus, however, we fortunately possess, in fifty-four books: each of which, says his English translator, Thomas Taylor, "is an oracle of wisdom and a treasury of invaluable knowledge."

I shall presently try to put before you a few fragments roughly broken off from the mass of wealth which these treasures contain, but before doing so it will perhaps be as well to finish this slight historical sketch of the Neo-Platonic school. Having studied philosophy for eleven years at Alexandria, Plotinus travelled into Asia with the intention of investigating the religion and philosophy of the Persians and Indians in their native homes. This purpose, however, he was prevented from carrying out by reason of the war between Rome and Persia, but his writings prove that he was acquainted with the wisdom of the East. In his fortieth year he came to Rome, where he resided thenceforward. The most distinguished disciple of Plotinus was Porphyry, a native of Tyre, many of whose writings remain to us, though many also are lost. Among the missing, unfortunately, is a book which would have had a great interest for us: his book against the Christians, which raised a terrible disturbance at that time. It is said that above thirty Christian authors wrote replies to it, some of them of very great length, and they called Porphyry all the bad names they could think of. And finally, though a long time after Porphyry was dead, the Christian Emperor Theodosius ordered the book to be publicly destroyed, and not a single copy escaped. We can judge of the book now only from certain extracts which have been preserved in the writings of Christian fathers. Porphyry seems to have made a distinction between the Christianity of Christ, and that of the Christian Church; and he declared that the Christians had perverted the pure doctrines of Christ; which was perfectly true. He attacked the authenticity of the Book of Daniel, and maintained that it was a spurious production, of much later date than that which was claimed for it. In this also, I suppose, many people would now admit that he was perfectly in the right. But the views of some of the more philosophical Christians, during those early centuries, were considerably coloured by Platonism.

To Porphyry succeeded a number of more or less distinguished Platonists, some of whom have left writings of high interest and value. But it is not necessary to recite a list of names. The greatest of the successors of Plotinus and Porphyry was undoubtedly Proclus, who was born at Byzantium in the year 412, and died in 485. Proclus, according to his biographer Marinus, was very particular about observing religious rites and institutions, not only of his own country, but of other nations as well. I do not think it can be supposed that he acted thus altogether from superstition, and it is quite certain that he was profoundly versed in the esoteric meaning and value of all these rites and institutions. But in the time of Proclus the ancient beliefs and philosophies were fast fading away before the advancing power of Christianity, Even before Proclus was born, the edicts of the Emperor Theodosius had let loose upon the empire, under the name of Christianity, a flood of barbarism and superstition. Those who adhered to the ancient faiths were insulted and persecuted, their rites were forbidden, their temples everywhere destroyed. When Proclus was yet a child, the light of the Platonic school of Alexandria, Hypatia, was murdered—torn limb from limb by a rabble of Christian monks. Porphyry was right: the Christians had indeed perverted the doctrines of their founder! The Gospel of peace and good-will had become in practice a well-spring of strife, of persecution, and of spiritual despotism. With the ancient religions, the ancient philosophy, or Theosophy—for what is philosophy in its highest form but Theosophy?—was also doomed. Its extirpation would doubtless have been more rapid had not the Christians been diverted by their innumerable internal dissensions. They hated each other even more than they hated the pagans. I think, then, that the minute observance which Proclus is said to have paid to the rites and formalities of the old religions can be attributed to no other cause than his desire to honour and publicly support them in this time of danger, and to his consciousness that in upholding this religion he was doing his best to uphold philosophy also against their common enemy.

The writings of Proclus are of the greatest value. The most important of those which remain are commentaries on the works of Plato, and it is almost impossible to get at the full meaning of Plato in the more occult parts of his works, unless we study them with the aid of these commentaries of Proclus. He was succeeded by several eminent Neo-Platonic philosophers. But in the reign of the bigot Justinian the persecution of the pagans became more acute, and the public teaching of philosophy was terminated when the Emperor closed the school of Athens in the year 529. A few of the ejected philosophers sought the protection of Khosru, King of Persia, who, says Taylor, "was the means of procuring for them an exemption from the barbarous penal laws of Justinian against the pagans; and thus enabled them to end their days in security and peace, and in the enjoyment of that liberty of conscience which no religion before the Christian ever attempted to destroy."

We have seen, then, that the school of philosophy to which the name of Neo-Platonic has been given, existed for a period of some 300 years, from its foundation by Ammonius, the porter, to its suppression by Justinian, the Emperor. I must now try to give you some glimpse, necessarily very inadequate, of the nature of that philosophy itself, and in doing so I shall draw my illustrations chiefly from the writings of Plotinus. According to that philosopher, the hypostases or principles of things are three: the One, Intellect, and Soul; and as Intellect emanates from the One, so also does Soul emanate from Intellect. We will attempt a brief investigation of these three principles, separately, and in their proper order.

The One, then, is that which is indeed incomprehensible, though it is called by many names. It is the First Cause, the hidden Deity, the Absolute, Parabrahm. But the Platonic philosophers refer to it chiefly by these two appellations—the One, and the Good; by *the One* denoting that Unity from which all things proceed; by *the Good*, "that supreme object of desire to which all things ultimately tend." And that impulse of the soul which causes it to return to the source from which it descended, is Love.

Damascius, one of the latest of the Neo-Platonists, has this analogy respecting the One: " he is truly an incomprehensible and inaccessible light, and is profoundly compared to the Sun; upon which the more attentively you look, the more you will be darkened and blinded; and will only bring back with you eyes stupified with excess of light." But although it is impossible to comprehend the One, it is nevertheless necessary to postulate it, as the source of all things. For it is evident that without the One, the *many* could not subsist; for, as Proclus says, if multitude did not participate of the One, neither would the whole be *one* whole, nor would each of the parts be *one* part, but the whole would be many wholes, and each part many, and so on *ad infinitum*. The One, therefore, is the source of all things, but it is no thing. It is not Intellect, nor Soul, nor is it even Being; for it transcends Being; it is One alone.

We come now to the second hypostasis or principle of Plotinus: *viz*., Intellect. But here it is necessary to premise that the word Intellect is used in a sense very different from that in which we commonly employ it. It is the Greek νοῦς—that which *perceives* itself—self-consciousness. Now it is clear that the One cannot be self-conscious; for self-consciousness implies a certain duality or even triplicity; there is consciousness itself, there is that which is conscious, and that of which it is conscious. Whereas the One, as we said, is One alone. But let us consider the Intellect—νοῦς—from this point of view. There is that which perceives, *viz*., the Intellect strictly speaking; that by which it perceives, *viz*., the Intelligence, and that which is perceived, *viz*., the Intelligible. But, evidently, the first thing which the Intellect perceives will be, that it *is;*

and therefore, the Intelligible is, primarily, Being, or Essence. Intellect moreover perceives that it is *not One*; since, if it were One simply, it would have no perception of itself. But it is One by participation of the One; for it emanates immediately from the One, and therefore participates more fully of the One than those natures do which are subsequent to itself. Intellect, then, is both one and many, or many in one; or, in the words of Plotinus, it is "a multitudinous impression of *the good* which entirely abides in unity." And again he says: "With the whole itself it perceives the whole, and not a part by a part."

"Now being two" (I am still quoting from Plotinus), "this *one* thing is at once intellect and being; intellective and intelligible. It is intellect indeed, so far as it is intellective; but being, so far as it is intelligible, or the object of perception to intellect. But intellectual perception could not subsist, if difference and sameness did not exist." That is to say, there is clearly a difference between perceiving and being perceived, although, in so far as the perception is *true*, there is also a sameness between perceiver and perceived; since *absolute* knowledge, which subsists on this plane of intellect, is nothing else than the identity of the subject perceiving, with the object of its perception. But to return to Plotinus :—

"It is likewise necessary to assume together with these [that is, with difference and sameness], motion and permanency. And motion indeed is necessary if being intellectually perceives; but permanency in order that it may remain the same; and difference in order that it may be at once intellective and intelligible. For if you take away difference from it, then becoming *one* it will be perfectly silent. It is necessary, however, that intellective natures should be different from each other; and that they should also be the same with each other, since they subsist in the same thing, and there is something common in all of them. Diversity, likewise, is *otherness*. But these becoming many, produce number and quantity. And the peculiarity of each of these produces quality; from all which, as principles, other things proceed."

Thus the intelligible world, which is all comprehended in this word Intellect, or Nous, comprises the intelligible (which is essence); intelligence (which is life); and the intellectual; sameness and difference; motion and permanency; and finally number, quantity, and quality.

"It comprehends in itself," says Plotinus, "all immortal natures, every intellect, every god, and every soul, all which subsist in it with invariable stability. . . All things that are there are perfect. Intellect perceives, not investigating, but possessing. It possesses all things in eternity."

And in another place he says :—

"Intellect is real being, and possesses all things in itself, not as in place, but as itself, and as being one with them. But all things there subsist collectively at once, and yet nevertheless they are separated from each other; since the soul also, which has many sciences in itself simultaneously, possesses them without any confusion. Each also, when it is requisite, performs what pertains to it, without the co-operation of the rest."

And once more:—

"Intellect is as it were the first legislator, or rather the law itself of existence. Hence it is rightly said, that it is the same thing to perceive intellectually and to be, and that the science of things without matter is the same with the things themselves."

To this part of our discourse, which deals with the subject of Intellect, belongs the consideration of the Platonic doctrine of Ideas. Ideas are defined as "the exemplary causes of things, which perpetually subsist according to nature." You know that this visible universe and all that it comprises—all *corporeal* natures, that is to say—are said to have no real subsistence of their own. They are merely images or reflections of something which has a real subsistence. Plotinus somewhere compares the forms which are in matter to a reflection in a looking-glass, which appears to possess form and substance, though actually it possesses nothing but the appearance; for the real thing, of which it is a reflection, is somewhere else—it is not in the looking-glass. Now this real thing, of which the whole visible universe is the reflection, subsists in the intelligible world; for the intelligible, as we have seen, is real being. This archetypal world, then, contains the ideas of all things, or rather, it *is* the ideas of all things, collectively and unitedly—the many in one. Corporeal natures reflect intelligible ideas: incorporeal natures participate them. Ideas, moreover, are permanent, because the permanent alone is real. Change, decay, and imperfection have no place in the world of ideas; for these things are the passions of matter, which is non-being. And change and imperfection are in incorporeal natures in so far as they are drawn to matter, and become assimilated to it, forgetting whence they came, and in what their true being consists. Thus there is an idea of good, but there is no idea of evil; since good is positive, while evil is negative merely, a defect or privation of good, just as darkness is a privation of light. And, to carry yet further this analogy, we say that Intellect is absolute light, and matter is absolute darkness or privation; while between Intellect and matter is Soul, proceeding from Intellect, descending into Matter, and again reascending to its parent, Intellect; and experiencing, during its course through time, every possible degree of illumination, from the perfect splendour of the liberated soul, to the dim twilight of the most degraded, trembling, as it were, on the very verge of nothingness.

With one more brief quotation from Plotinus, I will conclude what I have to say this evening on the subject of the second Platonic hypostasis:

"Intellect," he says, "is truly the maker and demiurgus. Matter, receiving forms, becomes either fire, or water, or air, or earth; but these forms proceed from another cause, and this is Soul. Soul imparts form (or appearance) to the four elements of the world; but Intellect becomes the supplier of productive principles to Soul; just as productive principles being inserted from the Arts in the souls of artists, enable them to produce works of art."

This leads us to the third hypostasis—Soul, of which Plotinus gives the following definition:—

"Soul is the reason or discourse (λόγος) of Intellect, and a certain energy of it, just as Intellect is of that first God who is beyond Intellect."

And in another place he says:—

"Although Soul is so great a thing, yet it is a certain image of Intellect. And just as external discourse (or speech) is an image of the discursive energy within the soul, after the same manner, soul, and the whole of its energy, are the discourse of Intellect, and a life which it emits as the principle or hypostasis of another thing; just as in fire, the inherent heat of it is one thing, and the heat which it imparts another."

Soul, then, subsists primarily in Intellect, and proceeds from it as the principle of the universe. Intellect, indeed, is the demiurgus, the creator, but it is through Soul that the work of creation is effected. In Intellect the universe subsists in reality, but not in appearance: Soul fashions the visible image, and fills it with life.

"For," says Plotinus, "just as the rays of the sun, illuminating a dark cloud, cause it to become splendid and golden to the view, thus also, soul entering into the body of heaven gave it life, gave it immortality, and excited it from its torpid state. . . . But before this, it was body without life; or rather, the darkness of matter and nonentity."

But Soul, as he says:—

"Does not give life to individuals through a division of itself into minute parts, but it vivifies all things with the whole of itself; and the whole of it is present everywhere, in a manner similar to its generator," Intellect.

Soul, therefore, like Intellect, is both one and many; and the one is many, and the many are one, and yet many. From the one Soul which is derived from Intellect proceed the soul of the universe and all the souls which are contained in the universe; and one essence is in all. And the capacity of the whole is in each; so that each soul is the one soul in capacity, though not in energy. For when Soul descends into a material nature, its energies are necessarily limited by the vehicle which it has made for itself. Nor, again, is it to be supposed that on quitting this vehicle, the body, the soul loses its individuality. We have seen that Intellect comprises in itself many natures, all united in one essence, yet each distinct in energy. Just in the same way, the Soul which proceeds from Intellect, comprises in itself many individualities, also one in essence but distinct in energy.

"Apart from bodily differences," says Plotinus, "souls differ, especially in their manners, in the operations of the reasoning power, and from previous lives. . . . All souls are all things, but each is characterized by that which energizes in each. This, however, is the same thing as to assert that one soul indeed is united in energy, another in knowledge, and another in appetite. Different souls also behold different objects, and are and become the very objects which they behold."

"But," says he in another place, "no being perishes. The intellects which are in the intelligible do not perish because they are not corporeally distributed into one thing; but each remains, professing in *difference* a sameness of subsistence, in which its very being consists. In the same way with souls: they preserve their sameness and their difference, and each remains one, and at the same time all are one. We have shown that all souls are from one soul, and that all of them are divisible and at the same time indivisible. The Soul also, which abides on high, is the one reason of intellect, and from this Soul partial reasons (or souls) are derived, in the same manner as partial intellects are derived from one Intellect which ranks as a whole."

These three, then—the One, Intellect, and Soul—are, according to Plotinus, and the Platonic philosophers in general, the hypostases or principles of all things. We will now take a brief glance at one or two further points of this philosophy, and in the first place, following the example of the soul, we will proceed to matter. Matter is defined by Plotinus as "a certain subject and receptacle of forms." That is to say, it has no objective existence, but it has a certain existence as the subject of form. For of itself matter has neither quality nor quantity: it is simply privation of being—non-being. And Soul, investing this non-being with forms which are the images of those true forms or ideas which subsist in Intellect, produces body—that is, an illusory appearance of being. There is, however, another kind of matter, which is the subject of true forms, and this matter pervades the intelligible world, just as that which we commonly call matter pervades the apparent or sensible world. But the intelligible world, as we have seen, is the world of real being, and therefore intelligible matter is essence; and, on the other hand, the sensible world is the world of illusion, and the matter which is there is non-being. Essence, moreover, is changeless; but the matter which is in generated natures is always changing its form. Thus matter is also defined as that which is always becoming, but never *is*.

The illusory nature of the visible universe is of course, with all Platonists, an essential article of their creed. But while admitting this to the fullest extent, they did not all think it necessary to despise the world on that account, or to shut their eyes to the beauty of its illusions. You know that the love of beauty was one of the great characteristics of the ancient Greeks. This national sentiment was shared by some of their philosophers, who perceived the affinity subsisting between external and internal beauty. In Plato's works, especially, the artistic feeling is easily recognisable. But even in Plotinus, one of the most mystic of the

Platonic philosophers, this sense of beauty was not wanting. "This world is an image of the intelligible," he says. "But what more beautiful image of it could there be?" And again he says: "His mind must be dull and sluggish in the extreme, and incapable of being incited to anything else, who on seeing all the beautiful objects in the sensible world, all this symmetry and great arrangement of things, and the form apparent in the stars though so remote, is not moved by the view, and does not venerate them as admirable productions of still more admirable causes." He even goes the length of saying that "nothing which is *truly* beautiful externally, is internally deformed. For everything which is externally beautiful, is so in consequence of the domination of inward beauty." And to those who adduce instances of evil souls inhabiting beautiful bodies, Plotinus says, that in such cases either the external beauty is *false*—not what he means by true beauty—or that the inward deformity is, as it were, adventitious, and results from some impediment which temporarily prevents the soul from emerging according to its better nature. It is a very difficult question, and we will not discuss it at present. But I suspect that by *true* external beauty, Plotinus means something more than mere correctness of form.

By way of conclusion, I propose to say a few words upon the great Theosophic doctrines of Karma and Reincarnation, as they are presented in the writings of the Platonists. The doctrine of Karma, indeed, we shall not find definitely formulated there as we have it in the writings of Madame Blavatsky, but it is certainly implied in the Platonic philosophy, and sometimes more than implied. There is a very beautiful allegory in the last book of Plato's *Republic*, concerning the influence of necessity and free-will in the life of the soul. Around the distaff of Necessity, he says, the whole Universe revolves; and within this mighty power each soul has a certain right of choice as what its future life shall be. But this choice of the soul is controlled, or limited, by the Fates, the daughters of Necessity; and their names are the Past, the Present, and the Future. And it is the Fate of the Past who grants, and controls, this power of choice in the soul; for she comprehends in herself both the present and the future. That is to say, our free will is bounded, our present actions and the whole of our future existence are directed by the course of our past lives. And this, as I take it, is the doctrine of Karma.

The later Platonists held the same doctrine. "Each soul," says Plotinus, "descends to that which is prepared for its reception, according to similitude of disposition. For it tends to that to which it has become similar." And again he says: "No one can ever fly from the punishment which it becomes him to suffer for unjust deeds. For the divine law is inevitable." That is, the law of Karma. He speaks also of the apparent injustice which is so frequent in human affairs, of the sorrows and misfortunes which come upon people, as it seems, through no fault of their own; and these things, he says, are the result of our own actions in a previous life. Thus he teaches reincarnation together with Karma, and these two doctrines are, perhaps, inseparable. But further, both these doctrines are again united in the teaching that we must suffer where we have sinned; that on whatever plane of existence the debt has been incurred, on that plane the payment also must be made. This teaching also we find in Plotinus. Souls that have bodies, he tells us, must be punished in the body. But souls that are pure—that have ceased to reincarnate—are "there where essence and being and that which is divine, subsist, *viz.*, in God."

The Platonists, indeed, always regarded the connection with body as a species of death to the soul. For matter being, as we have said, a privation of being, and body an illusion, it is evident that in so far as the soul is drawn to matter, and becomes engrossed with the affairs of the body, so far it recedes from real being and its true life. The soul, therefore, can be said *wholly* to live, only when it is entirely liberated from its sepulchre, the body. And this liberation is the work of the soul alone. It is by no means effected by the death of the body. Porphyry has these words: "That which nature binds, nature also dissolves: and that which the soul binds, the soul likewise dissolves. Nature, indeed, bound the body to the soul; but the soul binds herself to the body. Nature, therefore, liberates the body from the soul, but the soul liberates herself from the body." For the soul, then, which has not of itself severed the bonds which connect it with the body, the death of the body is no release. It must reincarnate, and again reincarnate, until the bond is loosened, and the purified soul, its long pilgrimage ended, is restored to its true home in the intelligible world.

"Many souls," says Plotinus, "who once ranked among men, do not cease when liberated from bodies to benefit mankind." Thomas Taylor was of opinion that Plotinus himself had incarnated solely for the benefit of mankind; and to those who have studied the writings of the great Neo-Platonist, such an opinion will not appear absurdly extravagant. After his death, Apollo's oracle declared him freed from the necessity of re-birth. And Plotinus himself appears to have had some presentiment of his approaching liberation. As he lay dying, a friend, whose coming had been delayed, entered the room. To him the philosopher addressed his last words: "I have been expecting you," he said; "and now I go to restore the divine part in me to that divine nature which flourishes throughout the universe."

W. E. WARD.

CPSIA information can be obtained
at www.ICGtesting.com
Printed in the USA
248895LV00007B